NATURE'S GROSSEST

VAMPIRE BATS DRINK BLOOD!

By Bert Wilberforce

Gareth Stevens
PUBLISHING

Please visit our website, www.garethstevens.com. For a free color catalog of all our high-quality books, call toll free 1-800-542-2595 or fax 1-877-542-2596.

Cataloging-in-Publication Data

Names: Wilberforce, Bert.
Title: Vampire bats drink blood! / Bert Wilberforce.
Description: New York : Gareth Stevens Publishing, 2018. | Series: Nature's grossest | Includes index.
Identifiers: ISBN 9781538209578 (pbk.) | ISBN 9781538209592 (library bound) | ISBN 9781538209585 (6 pack)
Subjects: LCSH: Vampire bats–Juvenile literature. | Vampire bats–Behavior–Juvenile literature.
Classification: LCC QL737.C52 W57 2018 | DDC 599.4'5–dc23

Published in 2018 by
Gareth Stevens Publishing
111 East 14th Street, Suite 349
New York, NY 10003

Copyright © 2018 Gareth Stevens Publishing

Designer: Laura Bowen
Editor: Therese Shea

Photo credits: Cover, p. 1 Bruce Dale/National Geographic/Getty Images; pp. 3–24 (background) Oleksii Natykach/Shutterstock.com; p. 5 Johner Images/Getty Images; pp. 7, 11 Dachs167/Wikimedia Commons; p. 7 (hairy-legged) Gerrycarter/ Wikimedia Commons; p. 7 (white-winged) File Upload Bot (Magnus Manske)/ Wikimedia Commons; p. 9 Nicolas Reusens/Moment/Getty Images; pp. 13, 19 Michael Lynch/ Shutterstock.com; p. 15 Michael & Patricia Fogden/Minden Pictures/Getty Images; p. 17 Oxford Scientific/Getty Images; p. 21 Westend61/Getty Images.

Printed in China

CPSIA compliance information: Batch #CW18GS: For further information contact Gareth Stevens, New York, New York at 1-800-542-2595.

CONTENTS

Boldface words appear in the glossary.

Creepy Creature

Bats are amazing animals. They're the only **mammals** that fly. Bats may seem creepy to us. The creepiest ones are called **vampire** bats because they drink blood! Should these bats give us **nightmares**? Read on to find out!

Just Three

There are more than 1,200 species, or kinds, of bats. Only three species drink blood. They're the common vampire bat, the white-winged vampire bat, and the hairy-legged vampire bat. They're found in Mexico, Central America, and South America.

common vampire bat

hairy-legged vampire bat

white-winged vampire bat

7

All vampire bats drink animal blood. The white-winged vampire bat and the hairy-legged vampire bat hunt animals in forests. The common vampire bat hunts farm animals. It doesn't happen often, but they do drink the blood of sleeping people!

9

On the Hunt

Vampire bats live in large groups in trees or caves. They hunt at night. To find food, bats make sounds with their mouth or nose. The sound travels until it hits something. Then, the **echo** travels back to the bats' ears.

11

The echo can tell the bat an object's shape and size and exactly where it is. That's enough to let the bat know if it's something tasty to eat. The bat lands near its **prey** and hops or crawls to it.

Drink Up!

The vampire bat has a special part on its nose that helps it sense where blood is flowing near an animal's skin. The bat uses its teeth to cut the skin of its prey. The animal usually doesn't even feel it!

15

The bat licks the blood that flows from the cut. The special spit of the bat keeps the blood flowing. How much blood does the bat drink? A common vampire bat can double its weight in one feeding! That's gross!

17

Deadly Pests?

Vampire bats usually don't harm animals by drinking their blood. However, they may spread a **disease** called rabies that can be deadly. Rabies can harm people, too. That's why people often think of these bats as pests.

Only Food

Vampire bats are the only mammals that drink just blood. That might sound gross, but they can't eat or drink anything else. Their bloodsucking **behavior** helps them stay alive! Do you still think these cool animals are scary?

GLOSSARY

behavior: the way a person or animal acts, or behaves

disease: an illness that affects a person, animal, or plant

echo: a sound that is a copy of another sound and is made when sound waves bounce off a surface

mammal: a type of animal that feeds milk to its young and that usually has hair or fur covering most of its skin

nightmare: a dream that frightens a sleeping person

prey: an animal that is hunted or killed by another animal for food

vampire: in stories, a dead person who leaves the grave at night to bite and suck the blood of living people

FOR MORE INFORMATION

BOOKS

Hirsch, Rebecca E. *Vampire Bats: Nighttime Flying Mammals*. Minneapolis, MN: Lerner Publications, 2015.

Kenan, Tessa. *It's a Vampire Bat!* Minneapolis, MN: Lerner Publications, 2017.

Niver, Heather Moore. *Vampire Bats After Dark*. New York, NY: Enslow Publishing, 2016.

WEBSITES

Common Vampire Bat
animals.nationalgeographic.com/animals/mammals/common-vampire-bat/
Read about the amazing mammal called the vampire bat.

Vampire Bat
kids.nationalgeographic.com/animals/vampire-bat/
See awesome pictures of these flying creatures!

INDEX